CHEMICAL TENDENCIES

CHEMICAL TENDENCIES

poems by
PAUL LIEBER

TEBOT BACH • HUNTINGTON BEACH • CALIFORNIA • 2011

© 2011 Paul Lieber. All rights reserved. No part of this book may be used or reproduced in any manner whatsoever without written permission except in the case of brief quotations embodied in critical articles and reviews.

For information, address Tebot Bach Permissions Department,
Box 7887, Huntington Beach, CA 92615-7887 USA.

Design, layout, cover design: Tania Baban-Natal, Conflux Press
Front cover art: Sam Lieber

ISBN 13: 978-1-893670-65-5
ISBN 10: 1-893670-65-1

Library of Congress Control Number: 2011928186

A TEBOT BACH BOOK

Tebot Bach, Welsh for little teapot, is A Nonprofit Public Benefit Corporation which sponsors workshops, forums, lectures, and publications. Tebot Bach books are distributed by Small Press Distribution, Armadillo and Ingram.

THE TEBOT BACH MISSION

Tebot Bach is dedicated to strengthening community, promoting literacy and broadening the audience for poetry by demonstrating through readings, workshops, and publications, the power of poetry
to transform human experience.

This book is made possible by a grant from The San Diego Foundation Steven R. and Lera B. Smith Fund at the recommendation of Lera Smith.

www.tebotbach.org

*For Gwenn, Sam
and in memory of Marlyn*

TABLE OF CONTENTS

*** 1 ***

- 11 Phil or Seymour
- 12 True
- 13 Slice of Life
- 14 The First Blackout
- 15 Yield
- 17 B & H Dairy
- 18 Directions
- 19 Cravings
- 20 The Tide Changes
- 21 Currents
- 22 My Optical Migraine
- 23 Take This Twice a Day and Come Back Friday (The '70s)
- 25 I Slurp Less Than I Used To
- 26 Cock
- 27 Yard Sale 2
- 28 $2000 for a Ringside Seat
- 29 The First Marxist President
- 31 The Rio Grande River is Sand (2001)
- 32 Loops
- 33 Outside Her Mind
- 34 Die
- 36 Preparation for an Endless foyer
- 38 Off Broadway
- 40 Commercial Audition
- 41 The Audition of Clouds
- 43 After Two Hundred-Fifty TV Shows, a Couple of Years on Broadway and Thirty Cents in My Bank Account
- 45 Acting Teachers
- 48 Another Mouth

*** 2 ***

- 51 Chemical Tendencies
- 52 Going In
- 53 Sam 4
- 54 Division
- 56 Notes Beside Me
- 57 The Unnoticeable Movement of a Cloud

58	Plays
59	Long Beach Aquarium
60	Allied Model Train Store
61	Sam, Birds and the Homeless
62	Everything Repeats Until It Doesn't
64	I Watch for Corners and Boiling Liquids
65	Sports Bar in Santa Monica
66	Almost Blues at Burton Chase Park
68	Shuffle at the Santa Monica Pier
69	Yard Sale
71	Chinatowns
73	Boned on Venice Pier
75	Los Angeles Museum of Natural History
77	Death Valley
78	Kenneth Hahn State Park
79	Mouse Trap
80	Someone Cut the Stem Off
81	Joshua Tree National Park

*** 3 ***

85	Sister
86	But Didn't Roy Orbison Die of Cancer
87	I'm Thinking of What's His Name
88	Like Lost Children
89	We Think
90	A Month to 6 Weeks More Like a Month
91	Frugality
92	I Fell Asleep and Then Woke and Remembered I Had A Terminal Disease
94	Jet Lag at the Funeral Home
95	But It's Solid Wood
96	How I'd Like My Funeral

98	About the Author
99	Acknowledgments

1.

Tom Seaver: Hey, Yogi, what time is it?
Yogi Berra: You mean now?

PHIL OR SEYMOUR

We have something to tell
you and I knew the serious-
ness because they never
had anything to tell
that they didn't just tell.
That grandmother of yours
who we said died
before you were born
is living at Rockland State
Mental Hospital.
I want to mention
how things explain
themselves eventually,
like mother's fishy smiles
when we talked about
grandparents or father
always handing coins to
gone women on the streets.
Next was the visit. We took her
for a drive. Dad was never
David, but Burt or Harry
and mom never Kate
though she repeated I am
Kate to Selma who was always
Selma in the front seat
of the Ford Fairlane between
father at the wheel and
mother's surrounding arm.
Grandmother was so friendly
with her perky mistaken names
and locations. I sat as Phil
or Seymour in the back seat
on the Lower East Side
of Manhattan in Long Island
and Warsaw. It was 1937—
before I was born.

TRUE

I have answers in my front pocket,
sneak a look at Ellen's uncovered

solutions, 7, 9, 11, blackened
true. A white silence and

I can't remember. I read a paragraph
about imports exports wholesale

retail exports retail export and
wholesale imports and am asked

the theme. The mind vacuums
a freckled shoulder and a couple

of beauty marks. The teacher moves
from desk to chair, oblivious to doubt.

Needles of fluorescence and I'm in the spot
light, so, give up on a fumble to the pocket

and gamble a straight line of false
then crisscross true false true,

bet false for 19 and 20. Two weeks
later Mrs. Shapiro asks if English

is spoken at home. I answer false.

SLICE OF LIFE

He caught me
by the refrigerator,
pouring orange juice,
said, *if a guy pulls a knife,*
plan on getting cut,
it's going to happen,
so plan on it, rip off your jacket,
shirt or whatever, quickly wrap it
around your shoulder and arm,
never fight him front,
just give him the side
where the wrap is.
He was pretty worked up,
sweating, repeating himself
as he tied handkerchiefs
and a banlan shirt around his arm.
It was not what I wanted
to hear, but he needed attention.
Mother alternately laughed and
warbled phrases like, *see what happens*
when he drinks, he gets nuts.
He pointed to the bone edge
between the pinkie and wrist,
explained, this was the hardest
then chopped at the wall
and cabinet above.
Glass pieces showered,
revealing layers of paint
under the yellow coat.
Twenty years of mint green
on sky blue on yellow again
with see-thru glass pane
at the bottom. For a few seconds
we marveled at our ignorance,
having thought the cabinet wood
all those years.... then on
to how you slice up someone
with a piece of glass.

THE FIRST BLACKOUT

The subway stopped. I was
midway up the stairs
and without blinking, lights faded
and the sky joined Union Square.
I headed to 134 east 17th
climbed five flights and how my father
showed up at the draftsman-kitchen-
table I don't remember, but there
he was as if to remind me he
was still my father and though
his role seemed as arbitrary,
as say, the unlit street lights,
he asserted, so it seemed,
that he was mobile and could appear
even after I had moved out,
even when transportation failed.
He brought his father fumes into
my incipient-bohemian-exposed-brick-flat
in his pin-striped-almost-solid
blue suit and solid tie, the one
my mother picked out.
He sat so comfortably and mocked
my neighbor who was mesmerized
by the Big Dipper also suddenly appearing.
How could his priorities be so perverse
as to put aesthetics before the
unexplained blackout that will cause
profound loss or signal an invasion.
It brought together unlikely clusters
in elevators, subway cars and in my apartment.
I'd lie if I said I didn't want him
there in candlelight.
I'd lie if I said I didn't want
him there, with me-
together,
together and helpless.

YIELD

She tells me
strangers yelled
for her
to jump in
a convertible
and she did head
for three stiff penises
and then
they drove her
to the penis
of their dog.

You can lose yourself in a hop or a turn.
This particular skid
happened
when her boyfriend took off
after four years of breakfast.

One departure leads to another.
Before you know it
there's no blood in the trees
and a voice comes from the sewer.

It's so friendly
when it chews
your intestines
you smile.

She goes on
as we head south
about all her indecisions.

Little does she know
I too could join traffic,
stumble off with pigeons
if they'd invite me.

Watch her lips move.
Watch them tell me what to do.

B&H DAIRY

I've chewed at this counter
for 25 years and for 25 years

customers knock my back,
shoulders, shuffling the narrows

and I swallow that with parsley hints
and thick lima beans and Leo, dead,

listened more than any father
while he chopped onions,

tomatoes, cheddar. Mark, Clyde,
Gwenn, Leroy, Joan, Vinnie.

Dave abused everyone at the register.
Gout bloated his foot 'til they cut it off

and he couldn't dodge loan sharks.
He's under Florida. A Jew no longer

owns the place, but the blintz is the blintz
and the noodle pudding still bounces.

The lady who told me I'll just die
when I eat the egg barley

is dead and death is jello without fruit
suspended, rice pudding without

raisins. A guy I don't know
bags my challah. I'll finish it tonight

before it crusts and hardens.

DIRECTIONS

Billy asks me to go down
to the village to kick the shit
out of fags and it seems original
similar to the first fins on a Chevrolet
or when Billy led me into his room
which lit into a different borough
when he showed his sketches of
Tony Curtis and Dean Martin
in charcoal, staring up at me
caught on rough tan paper.
We grab the D train to Washington Square.
A slender blond strolls toward the trucks
on Hudson near Christopher.
Billy punches concrete first and
then the guy's softer teeth
and this too is a lesson.
I've misled you because the beating was another night.
I've misled you because I wasn't actually there.
I mislead you because that's what people do
and though I might say
that same night I copied a picture
of Steve McQueen out of Life
and rushed up flights to show Billy
it too might have been a different night.

CRAVINGS

She begs to see penguins,
the monogamous penguins.
It's a baby's chant she resumes
from time to every time. So

we cab it to renovated
Central Park Zoo, where she eats
penguins like lemon meringue.
They stick on lips of rock

in loyal families. She perches
among these flightless birds,
speaks to them of a remedy
for arthritis. I too remember

his swivel when a feminine
morsel passed, on Sixth Avenue
or other crosswalks, eighteen years
ago before he flew away.

THE TIDE CHANGES

She's stuffed with vitamins, almonds,
applesauce and yogurt,
lost a brother, a husband,
a hip and last month a daughter,

halts at a stoop to regroup
but it's blanketed in snow
so she leans on the red shopping cart
she calls her *Rolls Royce*.

She walks so so slowly
and I'm chilled on the path
to the bank. It's the business
after breathing stops. We do it

admirably in counterpoint.
I jog to the corner of resentment
then back to her.
Down the avenue of

who-she-could-never-be
then back. She persists
in full notes, pauses at a crosswalk.
I lead her around an ice patch,

guide her at the rim
of traffic as the words of a friend
repeat under my hood.
You will love the things

you take care of.

CURRENTS

You can't deny
the bulky gray '49 Ford
with running boards
and slang,
my father, a brimmed hat,
saying *groovy* and *hep*
with the thick sound
of an outsider.

Those things on his mind,
the stakes of responsibility,
running him into postures,
into treads.
I couldn't laugh
because that's what he feared.

The grilled radio
had to be turned off,
otherwise you'd
drain battery juice
even though the engine was off,
even though he was wrong.
I'd ask where
did he learn this fact of electricity
and that was the end
of discussion.

MY OPTICAL MIGRAINE

I'm all eyes as mother unleashes
her monologue, almost animated

in a hospital bed. The crank of her song,
background as perch and angel fish

blink above. She talks of Etta and Etta's father,
my great grandfather and Jenny raped

again by a rabbi in Rumania. Old news
as one relative bleeds into another.

Her shame mounts once more
for having an aunt who ran a cat house.

Cousins of cousins and a brother
who is short and a lung specialist

weave into the drone while a flight
of glorious tints disappears into dials

and graphs that measure heart beats
below her stories. There are no faces

to these names and no names
for prisms of light born in her

dyed hair. My ailment of triangles
dances to chatter of cousin Dave's sweet

sister Doris who taught the tango
but can't remember her address.

TAKE THIS TWICE A DAY
AND COME BACK FRIDAY
[The '70s]

I pet her bull dog at Seventy-third
and Third. She laments my departure,
hands me her number. We pick up
under the red and black squares

in my living room, onto the foyer,
past the incinerator, onto
the posturepedic. Two days later,
pea size blisters where the stem

mushrooms. Ninth Avenue and
Twenty-sixth Street, the V.D. clinic
with familiar doctors. I grab
a seat among numerous crossed

legs. I'm led to the bright room
where the black efficient one
examines a row of pulled down
pants, recites, *gonorrhea, non-*

specific urethritis, syphilis, then
lifts my penis and pronounces,
herpes. I call the girl. She's
unapologetic, but agrees

with the diagnosis. You can tell
you have it by the sting. When
translucent, ready to burst, it spreads.
After the pop, it dries and it's safe

to poke around. I pass it to Deborah,
Susan, Rachel, Natasha. Natasha shares it
with Ed, Ed with Diane then
back to me. On to Bette

who doesn't mind and bathes
it in sunlight, but that therapist
wakes me out of a sound sleep,
defies me to explain pimples

to her fiancée. I answer inadequately
through coughs and images
of tulips on her two-piece bathing suit,
with flesh between, below

and above.

I SLURP LESS THAN
I USED TO

I avoid images of her
face, bed turns and
tomboy bounce.

No, no eye on the anus
or boysenberry
between tongues.
No naked runs on
Santa Monica Boulevard or
calls at 4 A.M.
in multiple voices saying
she is losing
her minds.

I'll get out of bed,
grind beans, drip
boiling water through
a white filter.

COCK

She talks like a girl,
not girly talk. It's a generous
considerate sound and
sports her frilled dress and heels
like incidentals, carries herself
as if those genitals
don't indicate a thing.
She's my son's girfriend and they are
tender.
I think about
touching those breast implants, running
my tongue up her legs but
her dick swings
like a chandelier
though it's taped to the inner thigh
somewhere.
It's that dick I can't
stop thinking of,
the scrotum and testicles
like a clydesdale's,
like a great dane's,
hanging there oddly with nothing to do,
ignored like those distant
mountains that irrigate
the lower plains.
I give her a Thai fan
and she says thank you,
opens it, waves the air
as if she's entitled
to the breeze
she creates.

YARD SALE 2

His suits swing on a rope
between parking signs, the wool

striped powder blue, the three-piece
seersucker. Featured above

on a telephone pole is his once
fashionable blazer. Everything shifts

in the Santa Ana winds. A cotton
gray shirt does a 180 in a gust,

as fast as his mood would
reverse. A friend sports my father's

wind breaker. We're smothered
in dads. His would bring adolescents

home to fondle. He knows the price,
says, *a buck*, to the man who

inquires about my dad's blue polo.
The man rolls it into a ball, tosses it

in a pick-up truck and drives off
as cool as commerce can be.

A guy asks how much for the cords.
I say, *two*. He says, *one,* and explains

he needs the difference for lunch and
adds that he donates the clothes. He

rambles on as if I'm invested
in the twists of his logic, as if I'm not

making up my own stories, saying
bon voyage to a dead father and

his blue polo, as if they could hear,
as if feelings were mutual.

$2000 FOR A RINGSIDE SEAT

The believer dances around
the ring not believing
one of Christ's children
bit his ear in a clinch,

in a hug between men,
but it's no surprise to me
or Christ that a half-inch piece
bounces on the canvas.

What is an ear?
A petal.
A flower.
A delicious flap.

A dried peach
we sometimes nibble
or blow temptation into.
On the lower east side

during the blackout
someone tried to sell me
a half dozen
for less than two dollars.

THE FIRST MARXIST PRESIDENT

She thought the swordfish
overcooked or butter turned rancid
but I remember fury
just sprang from space
or around his belly
until it shook
the bald head
into spit and bark.

We waited for the rest
pretended he never fisted walls.

Nights he carried sauerbraten and
knockwurst above his head then
overcharged drunk Germans
who didn't add up. Afternoons
he tended bar. Pearl clouds
adorned the handles
of switchblades he ripped off
rowdy drinkers. They piled
on the dresser next
to the cuff links. He'd back
the knife and owner
out on Nostrand Avenue.

Mornings he'd lie
blubber dead under
quilts of bitter smells.
Coins sagged pants pockets
hanging on door corners.

In the thirties he ran with the party.
Saw a photo of him sitting cross-
armed and linked to other men
with grievances. He would never
mention the missing
finger or jail.

On Sundays we learned to listen
as if we listened while he
crayoned oil conspiracies on
paper napkins. Red faced
he'd bury Rob Roys
convinced for a second
of solidarity
on the other side
of a kitchen table.

THE RIO GRANDE RIVER IS SAND
(2001)

To my right is another drug store
with small white lines of anything
over the counter. It's two in the morning
at four in the afternoon.
I want to say something about
the look of these men as they stare
down women. I'll pick the words
raw, forlorn, and *ache.*
Toss them in any order you like
like the dirt that changes
to pavement then back to dirt
on these streets where a lack
of traffic lights scrambles everything.
A tin garbage can, upside down,
covers a smaller hole.
This town erases errors,
blends my torso with dry hills.
The signs read, *Juarez Mexico,*
but it's the Casbah or Avenue B,
ten blocks of familiar hustle
to the Tragadero Restaurante
where meat comes in tiny pieces
with white cheese on top
served at a long table
under portraits of local bull fighters.
Margaritas are a special 99 cents
so I buy for a new friend who speaks
more languages than I.

LOOPS

There was a guy on a talk show
who said he ate eighteen bicycles.
He chewed on a blue Schwinn
during the interview. You could
hear the crunches. The Raleigh
in front of me has a round chrome
bell on the left handle bar, the size
of a dumpling. Two of my friends
were crushed on bikes, one by a truck
on Ninth Avenue, the other sandwiched
between a double parked car and
bus. I count at least fifteen gears
on this one. The pedals at twelve
and six o'clock. It's all silver and black
with reflectors on the spokes.
I was a pall bearer for Jimmy, who like most
cadavers, didn't look himself. They put him
together with a never-knew-what-hit-me-
gaze. The seat on this one is a sweet
synthetic leather. I too coast
on top of two wheels, in love
with the wind and the contours
of the road that dance up my body.
Like any love affair, it can spin out.
The art coop gave Bette's
paintings away. I got the one
with the orange blob flowers
dangling in space, unattached
to the stems.

OUTSIDE HER MIND

She offers truffles,
says the one that doesn't look good
is, so I consume that one.
She cuts the cake I brought,
French chocolate from Claude's
and a peach tart, prepares tea
and she's thin spice ginger
mint. You enter the face
from the front, pour your soul into
the pale cavities, bone pressed
into fine cheeks. The eyes
recede into blue continents.
She talks of the usual,
Russian literature, how she coached
so and so and so I say
you look great and she replies
would you say I didn't ?
She's ninety-three and you'll never ask
if I wanted her. You'll never ask
because I'm forty years younger
and always have been. Forty years
are a few ticks on a fraudulent clock,
the faintest of sounds.
A corridor.
A collection of breakable china.

DIE

It's a two story red cube
on the south side
of a dark glass building
on lower Broadway
and we stride briskly,
the painter and I,
across Houston Street,
a left on Lafayette,
gaining speed as we get
closer, the way you
might hustle to a waterfall.

She talks of monkeys
and small erections
but conversation
switches to these lines
of Noguchi's and
what we understand.

I'm thinking how
she paints with people,
but all I can do is stand
next to the cube,
balanced on a corner,
part of her landscape
and sure it's sublime
when she splatters me
with her eye.

I tell her I don't know
if it's copper or steel
and what about the cylinder
cutting a diagonal?
Her head finds my shoulder,
catches the cube horizontally.

It's the draw of six sides.
It's the guile of right angles,
this scoop of a cube,
like red lipstick
on something alive.

PREPARATION
FOR AN ENDLESS FOYER

I'm sitting on wood in a courtroom.
Deep clear voices convince.
Two gray suits turn papers
on both sides of the table.
I want their everyday feel,
their strut and sure sound.

That's all I ever wanted.

My wifes' breasts swell.
Her belly distends
and neither one of us
believes.

Wednesday I'll play a lawyer,
April, a father.

The prosecutor
whispers into an ear.
This is the entry to his character.
A patch of plaid. A zipper.
A cardboard box.

They showed us
a blurred negative
of a charcoal head
and a curling spine.
The doctor put a mike
to my wifes' stomach
and there was a beat,
fast and loud.

In six months three of us.
I'll pick up an inflection
and fake the rest.

OFF BROADWAY

Mike the director blames
Gilbert, and Leo will never
work with Gerald again, while
Gerald fixes his wig for an hour
and sighs about everything
but particularly complains
that Jack hits him too hard
in their kidding around
fight scene. Leo used to blame
Clarence, thought he would sink
the ship while Clarence
mocks Gerald, and both
he and Leo bet which inanity
Gerald will say when he returns
to the dressing room after
Act one. Steven thinks Clarence
is a horrible actor though Leo
argues he is improving.
Jack is homophobic
so detests Gilbert who sings
show tunes backstage though
the play we are performing
is serious and everyone
watches out for Tanya who
is capable of ripping your balls
off on stage but is well behaved
but secretly complains to Dorothy,
the producer, about Mike.
Mike asks me to stand by him
when the shit flies, while
Stuart, the other producer
wants to fire Tanya, but Dorothy

believes in her. Stuart
loves me and gives me free tickets
but I can't tell Gilbert, Leo
Tanya, Gerald, Steven or Clarence.
The Times hates the play but
likes me, Steven and Leo
so the show closes even though
Joanne Woodward loves it
and everyone except for Gerald.

COMMERCIAL AUDITION

Jeremy David, Bunny Lane with prop glasses,
Ann Perry, and others, on shelves, in bins and
they might as well wiggle like worms, like bait,
tempting us with the spirals of their personalities

as I glimpse bleached teeth, almost hear the anecdotes,
piled on one another, random invitations to lunch or a chat.
I don't want to make this more grim than it is, this sale
for a sale, no, just 8x10 photos, discarded, stacked

and on their way to the trash. I'll probably never
meet Jeremy David, but maybe there is a Jeremy Junior
in his lap this very moment as they watch their favorite
commercial where the protagonist trips, gets nervous and blares out

an embarrasing something so they laugh hysterically
until Jeremy smothers Jeremy Junior, but wait,
this is an episode of "Law and Order" that follows
the commercial that paid the network that paid "Law and Order"

that would pay me and I would participate in this engine
of real-make-believe with my convincing foibles and homicides.
My name is Paul and that name is suddenly called. I'm
led into a studio and told to play a karate instructor

demonstrating the chopping of a brick to a group of kids
not here. I'm mean and intimidating until Captain Crunch,
also not here, enters and reduces me to a grovel of pleading
to be "crunchified." All this is put on tape to be viewed

by the cereal executives whom I'll probably
never meet, never know the allure of names their parents
gave them after a grandparent, an uncle
or perhaps an adored actor or actress, yes,

the very ones they printed on their resumes
to secure these responsibilites.

THE AUDITION OF CLOUDS

The bulbous double decker cloud moves
so slowly you wonder if it moves at all,
but come back in an hour
and it will be in another place,
replaced by sky, by nothing,
by another cloud.

And the audition
came on so suddenly,
made it clear
no matter how
make-up makes
a younger you,
you are still you,
the older you, always-
getting-older you,
piling on minutes
as you cover a rash.

A cluster of seconds,
of hours. It's Tuesday,
July 11, 2009.

You're in the right place.

Under the powder,
those stationary clouds,
the illusory ones
convince you you're the same,
still dazzled
by Clifford Brown, Billy Holiday
and the jump shot.

The voice attempts
to reassure,
clings, really,
with a murmur
on the precipice
of the waiting area
where others
resemble grandparents.
Some showcase their sag,
some tennis trim, but

the singular storm

tosses us here,
the gray couple,
"kvelling" over
their performing grandson…

No words, just fake glee
and fake affection
for my fake wife
who sits next to the fake me.

AFTER TWO HUNDRED-FIFTY TV SHOWS, A COUPLE OF YEARS ON BROADWAY AND THIRTY CENTS IN MY BANK ACCOUNT

This agent boasts he booked an actor
on The Sopranos, "top of the show,"
which is little to call attention
to in this billion dollar industry,

but we're in a mini-mall
with a sign posted LICENSED AGENCY.
The door cracks and his partner

enunciates each syllable of

*excuse me can I have that FEATURE
on your desk,* as if it's rehearsed
and they might as well peddle fake
rolexes or sucker me in a shell game.

The agent says he's connected to everyone,

asks if I know a comedian, a Kelly
Somebody, he represents, who did
a series in London, *bigger,*
more innovative than Mary Tyler Moore.

I remain seated because of the view
of snow lapping the San Gabriel Mountains,
the flow of his see-thru sell
and where would I go anyway?

We're threads in a gaudy fabric.
Can you feel it stretches across
our mouths, colors our words

then taints the Pacific? Outside
my manager knits the apology,
*what did I get you into what did I get you
into,* and tells of a client

and his film that's heading
for the Sundance Festival.
She lets out a cheer for him,
a cheer as she leaps
on Ventura Boulevard.

ACTING TEACHERS

Harris teaches, *never never improvise.*
Do you think Spencer Tracy
improvised? Joan is all
about improvisation. *Say what*
comes to you, own it, surprise
us, yourself, your scene partner.
Keep it fresh.

Mira teaches to accept the situation,
not create it. Milton urges to
attack the situation, add a twitch
or an occasional yelp.

Bill doesn't teach much of anything,
just praise the good and the bad will
dissolve.

Alice explains *substitution.*
Play it as if you were
with your lovely sister
or hateful aunt. You can almost
see them up there with you.
Harris mocks *substitution,* says, *just*
imagine. Never substitute. It's cheap
and you will always portray the same
character. Do you think
Spencer Tracy substituted?

Mira gives line readings that
aren't line readings, more
to get at the intent,
something that never ever changes.
Charlie's famous student
purposely changes line readings.

It keeps him on his toes.
Uta and Lee are dead against line readings
for any reason.

Sandy wants you to react
to your scene partner,
let him or her affect you.
He has you repeating their words
with their inflection
then your reaction.
That's his technique.
It's everything.
Mira counters,
two wrongs don't make a right.
Don't be swayed by
your untalented misguided
partner, work from the text.

Walt repeats, *work with your object.*
Tie that shoe lace, scrub that dish.
It will free you. Uta chimed, *add*
an obstacle like you can't find
the shoe. Hide it somewhere.
then forget where, and look for it.
Mira declares, *objects are unnecessary!*

Alice never went on stage without a tooth
ache. She creates it with sense memory.
Mira, Harris and Stella laugh
at sense memory. Lee and Charlie
swear by it.

Lee asserts that relaxation is the big
key and when I see him perform he
seems relaxed enough, but his lines
almost sleep. Flaccid sounds without
meaning.

George Burns says, *when you knock
on a door and the person inside says
come in, the good actor enters
and the bad one waits outside.*

ANOTHER MOUTH

The fragile green primitive
tooth was pried with reason

jimmied. A forty-percent chance
it could have been saved

but I opted for the yank
and now the space it filled   the space

my tongue is emotional about
explores like my mother's shy dog

timid of the strange   unsure
of the gap's meaning   it returns

to the other side of the mouth
the contours   the line of

smooth crowns   like tiny
familiar tombstones. It tries

to relax but this flap of flesh
suspects   it's just beginning.

2.

*"From what has come
Where come from—
New born babe."*

*"Will he know us
when he's come,
will he love us."*

— Robert Creeley

CHEMICAL TENDENCIES

Organic tomatoes, carrots, basil,
a clove of garlic and pasta
reduced in mother's milk
create a belching mass,
a hiccup,
a six-pound-seven-ounce reflex
on the other side of a nipple.
I'm free to deconstruct him
as he does me, views me
in black and white in a motion
with a gruff soundtrack
while I consider
my   son   thinking
hi m mi ne that the low er
lip similar as everyone says
and the turned up nose
my wife's. I deconstruct a
pretty *pe ni s* if you touch
it pops up and the proportion
of his feet and hands. Gargantuan.
He sleeps that pink sleep
with a sudden cry   a splash
of paint, the acid of tomato
looking for a way out.

GOING IN

His neck is longer
this morning and
the profile is almost
a regular thin boy.
He's eleven days
old and he grows
in my arms. There
are grimaces and
silent aches as a finger
stretches. He's
moving toward a thought,
toward a longer leg.
It's all temporary,
this unbreakable gaze
between us. Going in,
I'm careful with
these looks, too careful,
as if to protect
knowledge of me
he may already have.
This isn't a lesson
or sound philosphy.
It's something sad
like shyness,
like my mother
refusing a scotch
or my father
having another.

SAM 4

The wrist, milk chubby
the stomach, full of mild churning.
Notice the calf.
Stay a few minutes
until you kiss it also.
Explain to yourself that
you're your animal now,
sniffing his biceps, neck and flat ears.
Rub your nose into his soft skull.
Place him in a sling
on your chest. Quick breaths
match yours two to one.
His sleep wins you further over,
breaks you in pieces,
puts you back together
responsibly,
thinking I'll dig ditches,
become a UPS man.

DIVISION

I head for the unabridged
Webster's to look up *foreskin*.
It's a terminal fold that covers
the crown. Although he's cut
twelve thousand, I'm concerned.
Is it as definable as an ear lobe,
a lower lip? If there is a slip
will it separate my son
from a piece
of sentient flesh,
a rush
of blood?
The rabbi, slash, mohel
rolls his sleeve to explain,
the penis, his wrist,
a Ralph Lauren sleeve, the foreskin.
I'm saying *rabbi show me
again* until I don't know who
suggests we depart friends,
waiting the ritual,
into the alcove where he says
let's see the goods
with a glimmer for a grown-up
penis. I pull mine out and
he points to a slight pink line
lassoing the stem,
a safe distance,
a relief
from more sensitive spots.
I ask about the scar at the tip.
He says, *oh, everyone has that.*
For forty years this error
was my covenant with God.

Things fall into a place
when a gauze of red Manischewitz
kisses my son's lips and eyes
register a sweet distraction
from the swift clean slice.

NOTES BESIDE ME

the swerve of a nose
the flip of the line
into the soft plain of cheek
roll of lashes
pink and pink
and red blond fuzz
the form of a snore
behind a puff of lips
that seal a grown-up sound
a slight hiccup
my wife drops
into the clinic
I buckle him in
beside the whish of traffic
his inhale is an eighth note
a tightness in her chest
maybe it's the weaning
maybe it's the weight
of carrying Sam
or maybe the heart
so clenched and tied
to their routines
he's a cluster of azaleas
sleep murmurs
just above the earth
no one told me
really told me
about anything

THE UNNOTICEABLE MOVEMENT OF A CLOUD

He pinches my chin,
babbles, and it could bloom into Arabic,

Chinese or English. I heard, *I live you dada*
in elongated porous metallic chirps. Someone

told me all babies sound alike at six months
before they fall into language. Out of the blues

into accuracy. I remember I'd lean into ivory,
play dissonance with all the feeling of something

almost soft and melodious, before piano lessons,
before scales. At one A.M. I walk the length

of the living room, his head on my heart to remind
him when he curled near a similar beat. I march

back and forth. At fifty-two his legs hang
to my hips and arms are limp. At eighty-five

I crawl back in bed, complete. My wife embraces him
and he sticks to her milk smell. Years ago

an autistic child would say, *let's laugh together*
and we would, at nothing in particular,

at first forced, and then it would erupt
into the unstoppable gales of hyenas. My son

wakes, kicks his feet in opposite directions,
head leans back, back arches in a stretch

as he chants in nascent Portuguese.

PLAYS

He slides a plastic coffee top
on the table close to the back door
we opened to watch rain.

He's in my lap and I use him
with each greeting. *He's so cute,
perfect*, and they almost look at

me with these overtures.
I use him to explore puddles
outside, their short lives.

The stationary tongues of the ceilng fan
capture his gaze. I use him
to rethink circles and metal.

The patrons are mostly realtors,
lawyers. I'm here to catch money sense,
overhearing the shifts of value.

These people are not dead, but blink
and wave. A "reconstructed" blonde
grabs Sam's coffee top, returns it.

Her pale skin, pulled like his, she
repeats and we're all playing. I
lean for a sock that drops on the

floor, rise to smell artificial flowers.
I slice an avocado that he eats at a pace
I associate with sleep.

I use him to drift, to dig a well
of me. I apologize to the mouth,
to the table, to the spoon.

LONG BEACH AQUARIUM

A blown-up bass tunnels toward Sam,
mimes something about the art
of swiveling, appears to invite him

for a swim, but Sam runs in his own pool
of impulses, zigzags up a corridor to
slithers of silver, knifing through a smaller

tank in schools, around and around,
not too different than the mobs of Fifth Ave.
with fashion pinching their skins. *They*

are called anchovies, I hear one mother
emphasize, as if a word is equal to a swirl
of spines. Fish from the sea of Cortez

and the Bering Strait shine in multiple paisleys
and stripes, every which way. Sam shrieks
among the sharpest blues and yellow tails

with eyes set in the abstract pattern
that gather by a coral reef. A flatish fish, a wrasse
in lightest green-gray polish glides across.

I'd like a shirt that tone and a sweater like
that woven eel thing that entwines with sand.
A worker in black rubber and fins, bubbliing

under water, waves. I tell Sam we came from
a larger tank and he almost stills for a flash as jellyfish
parachute into the frame.

ALLIED MODEL TRAIN STORE

Trains the size of fingers or
thin thoughts that wind through
mountains speckled with moss.
A woman the width of a few hairs sits
on the step of a passenger car
for an overview. I spot cows
grazing, casting their miniature glances,
but Sam scurries to an industrial town
in browns and stained blacks.
A diesel crosses a bridge above
a glaze that suggests a river
that almost reflects our trance.
Behind a wide manufacturing building
where no train approaches
are people dressed for work
with brief brief cases. It's a street
that sanctifies the gait, the sitting position,
the mingle below lean lamps,
a tiny soppy eulogy, an aerial view
of the corner-wait-for-the-light-to-change.
It's a configuration I passed in New York
off route 17, the curve, that closed plant—
or was it Louisville near the defunct
slaughter house and the lingering
smell? Sam jigs and yelps
along side the locomotive
that reinvents us as it emerges
from a tunnel, then sprints to the turn
of the century. A steam engine,
a contraction of cylinders,
chugs between horses, cowboys,
and a stage coach. Linns' Laundry
is vacant. Small's Saloon draws
a crowd, but I'm cautious.
I could be lynched in this town.
I feel the tiny frowns and barks
about privacy and intrusion.
We don't check in the Parker Hotel.

SAM, BIRDS AND THE HOMELESS

He chases seagulls
and pigeons at Muscle Beach
where one man stretches
and the homeless
line the bleachers,
eating out of paper bags.
They egg Sam on,
get em, you can do it, get em.
Sam charges a bird
and the group laughs,
knowing he'll never
catch one, knowing
what's not possible.

EVERYTHING REPEATS UNTIL IT DOESN'T

He jumps at the sight
of a red steering wheel
that drives nothing in this playground,
reaches for the outline,
turns it with difficulty.
Back and forth,
it shifts in inches.
There's a pinwheel
behind his eyes.

The toy truck is upside down.
With one finger he rotates a tire.
He grabs the cap on the sun block,
twists, later flips
his baby carriage
and does two wheels at a time.

At the airport he
wobbled into a bar
toward three ceiling fans.
His 28 inches stared up at the spin,
atoms looking at atoms.
I lifted him toward his fascination.

He reinvents or remembers
something as he fixates
on the twirl.

I swivel my head on its axis,
follow him toward a hubcap.
Planets orbit. Everything turns,
repeats, my neck pain,
the lure of a breast.

This morning these empty swings
and slides are still
but we know that's an illusion.

I WATCH FOR CORNERS AND BOILING LIQUID

He's in one entrance,
out the other, gives a soft
high five to a patron
in blue leather and
I follow the intricate
engine that halts
at the cardboard box
brimming with onions
to handle, grabs a lemon
from another carton,
shuffles at the screen door
to signal me to open,
makes a sharp left to the patio
up to a dog the size of a stallion.
The horse washes his face.
He spins to catch
a gravelly voice
eating scrambled eggs,
pronounces himself
in front of the woman
who says, *hello what's your name?*
and I answer, *Sam*
as if we are the same.
He eyes a red bicycle helmet,
the colored anything
they wear,
slides into their moments
as naturally
as this breeze
that brushes with nothing
to say, but I'm here stranger,
you're there,
we can't hide in this cafe.

SPORTS BAR IN SANTA MONICA

We're cocked at a video game
where you race at top speed
in the city of your choice.
I select New York. Sam in my lap,
drops two quarters and we're off
past a sign that reads Cross
Bronx Expressway, above
the neighborhood I grew up in.
We're doing ninety around a slum
as we skid into the opposite lane,
crash, flip and although land upright
and poised to continue, Sam
screams the way he did when
a wide-jawed dinosaur came our way
in another game. We depart
the steering wheel to settle quietly,
hockey on a big screen, one fellow
wedged and elbowed by another,
on a smaller screen football players
pile up. Sam points to one picture,
says, *hockeee*, to the other, says,
futbaall, then mouths, *poool*
as he indicates the pool table
to the right with its round mindless
characters, also numbered,
making that pleasant ping
as their colors collide.

ALMOST BLUES AT BURTON CHASE PARK

The blues singer
feels too much
on this peninsula where no sound
is out of reach.
Boats silently padddle
or sail by.
Sam rolls down
a mound of green
in this fabricated park.
A collection of masts
pricks the sky
from the docked boats
around us.
A constant ripple
reminds me
of the ways of water,
the ability to handle
cross currents,
disagreements,
antagonisms.
Their fluid arrangements.
This singer screeches
for a note
and a lover
who left. My wife
and I don't talk,
but circle
as Sam sips
from each fountain.
We lift him
to catch the arc.
Pelicans nose dive
for fish we can't see.

This place is beefy
with tattoos, the old kind
with Mom, Sally
and other loyalties
cut into biceps
before the feuds.
Sam finds his way
to the stage, turns to his
mom and they settle
fifty yards from me.
I can live with this distance,
this spired oasis, a blue backdrop
of water and between us
only a hill of landfill.

SHUFFLE AT THE SANTA MONICA PIER

Sam picks up a gum ball
from a spiral quarter machine,
boots it to the tip of the pier
where fog thickens into a blur

of beginnings. A roller coaster
and ferris wheel loop into
clouds. There's my father
hanging on the wooden neck

of a stallion on a souped-up
merry-go-round forty-five years ago
and me thinking how awkward
he looked clinging to life

and now I see him off
the carousel where his past
clinged, played him
like a carved thing.

Sam slides into a chariot.
I almost fit beside him.
He says, *nice black horse*
and around it goes

YARD SALE

A stranger
fingers my tripod.
I say twelve bucks
because my friend
whispers twelve.
Why not twelve?
I took five for my
father's blue leather jacket
that I wore in another city.
I said, *take care of it,*
it was my father's
as if a dead father
is like all dead fathers.
I could have used twenty
but I wanted him to think
I'm above commerce.
A Latino woman
reaches for quarters
for oval glasses
and I make up a story
for each quarter
about the condos she cleans.
I can't divide business
from deep pockets
of sentimentality.
A girl Sam befriended
who sells paintings
that don't sell
selects my wife's
never-worn-black-silk-shirt,
six green-flowered cups and
a Chinese scarf.

I blurt, *one dollar*
for the way Sam
pronounces her name
when he looks for her,
when she can't be found
and he repeats,
where's Asu?
Where's Asoooo?

CHINATOWNS

Chipped, smirched, slanted,
four horses the size of rodents.
Sam mounts the greenish one

seriously concentrating on the whirl
of this merry-go-round that leaks
a tin melody, *I've Been Working*

on the Railroad. We're in Chinatown
in the spill of faded colors
among the what's-left-behind.

I'm thinking of the Bronx as
old folks sip tea in the company
of boarded shops, back

with grandmother, abandoned
in a borough just above
the draft of small-time deals.

My cousin punished himself
with a window-left-wide-open
in winter when he didn't study.

Those icy breezes
inflicted a Ph.D. and a ticket out.
Sam's not interested

in the *Liquidation Sale of Jade*

but searches for a penny arcade,
checks back rooms, alleys
barges into a club of mahjongg players

who never look up. I've mixed up
L.A. Chinatown with Chinatown
in New York where you drop

a dime to heat a griddle to force
a chicken "to dance," a cultural leap
next to pinball. I crouch eye level

to apologize. *There's no pinball
here.* Sam leans into a pond
where gold fish sneak a view

through grime and tosses
three pennies in.

BONED ON VENICE PIER

Latinos yank croakers out.
This one weighs about a pound,
swims in desperate circles
in a bucket that Sam

peeks in, grasping my thigh,
says he looks cute and asks
why he's there. The fish answers,
ayuda me! Ayuda me! And

I'm not ready to translate.
Sam inquires why a sardine flips
around. He's seen me gobble
beheaded ones, but not wiggling

on the ledge of this pier
like the doomed young girls
dancing to a boom box. Last night
a man was about to slice

me when my kicks woke my wife.
I flailed those fins of mine
while the rest of me
froze in the waters of a dream.

Families grill bass, leopard shark
fresh out of the infested bay,
camp in tents and joke
as their rods line up

waiting for a nibble.
These fish are bilingual and
I jabber in tongues,
reflexively lying,

casting tales of omission
into the ocean
of Sam's eyes
as if I never

pulled a frog's leg
off, stuffed raw salmon
in my mouth or wanted
to be skinned alive.

LOS ANGELES
MUSEUM OF NATURAL HISTORY

If museums had museums
for museums
this one would be there
where blank eyed grizzlies

balance on two legs while
coyotes corral their young
lit in the huge hall
that Sam charges down

to tackle the stationary
water buffalo. Animals
pose sixty years strong
against scrims of peeling rivers

lagoons and the smudge
of mountain tops.
The floor is a thousand cork squares
that Sam and I skip on.

I can't help but think of incisions.
What did they stuff baby caribou
with? What chemicals stiffen
these thirsty young ones?

If I could make a diorama
it would be my father taking
a strap to me in say, Yosemite.
Both of us bloated with down

a waterfall brushed behind
mom in her striped two-piece
mouth open, saying something
we never hear

while sister combs
her sun bleached hair, eternally, the silver buckle
descends. In fairness
it should catch father's awkward stroke

as he funnels rage into
a belt he couldn't find
into a whip-like motion
he probably only saw in films.

I have no idea why
I'd put it on display
if not to hint at deeper offenses.
It was the day we were going to a museum

but I preferred the front
of a twelve-inch screen
where Chief Pontiac and his band
of Indians circled the cavalry

wanted to watch horses
flags and rifles, painted bodies
and feathers bloodlessly
buckle over, then trampled, but

back to these bones
the tyrannosaurus reassembled
and Sam more interested in
jiggling his legs, arms, neck

and the rest of those parts
intact, pink and I can almost
see the flow of blood
where veins come close

to the surface, so close.

DEATH VALLEY

Salt, azurite, sulfur
turn into papier mache
mountains and rust
is a shadow, a red drift
we climb with a canteen
before breakfast,
before our time,
after moisture left.
A path calculates others
with appetite.
We sing off-key Beatle tunes
to the marble underpinnings
of our earth.
Sam bends
to blow a flower open.

KENNETH HAHN STATE PARK

Charlie screams a steady high shriek
on the monkey bars because he wants to go first.

Sam won't give up the tennis ball that Charlie
craves. Neither has learned the rewards of sharing

say…oil rigs with sand boxes. Kenneth Hahn
bequeathed this spread and I offer little to these

tiny souls opposite prehistoric-looking pumps, these
hungry Calder sculptures. I teach them to cough

into a handkerchief, shake pebbles from their shoes
and how to stick to a path to avoid a sudden tumble

into other fractures. We inhale deeply as if breezes
are innocent, climb the sounds of a stream until

we hit the massive view where downtown juts up
like a pink hallucination. Steel towers multiply

behind us like thin tumors and what's outside
will be inside as fishermen pull trout and catfish

from a man-made-natural-enough-looking lake
stuffed once a month. Sam and Charlie count trout

that gasp and flip on a brown paper bag. They
argue whether there are three or five.

MOUSE TRAP

Only the tail shows, a thin question mark,
so still, there is no doubt its vitals are

crushed by the little black house of a trap
with a pea of organic peanut butter

at its core. It's the third in two days
and my son wants to carry their limp bodies

to the pet store where they might
rise and join other little characters

turning wheels and spinning miniature devices
in that village on display, but we bury him

below egg shells in a plastic garbage bag.
It's a success, this murder. One starts small,

turn a curious hungry rodent into
a furry glove as lifeless, say,

as the space between people,
between Sam and myself,

the one that never gets bridged,
no matter how far we reach

into an explanation. Sam saw it dash
behind his toy train. He ran to imitate its run

and now lies still to imitate its stillness. He rises
to watch Ciberchase on ABC.

SOMEONE CUT OFF THE STEM

The last time it happened
a few days later
they stripped the rear tire.
In Manhattan I'd set

my Raleigh in view,
entrapment of sorts,
thinking I'd pummel
the thief, thinking I needed

a reason to pummel
someone...anyone.
But when the seat
vanished today

I heard myself say
to Sam, *they needed it
more than I did.* I'll just
leave the bicycle

until the handle bars, brakes
and the rest
disappear and all that's left
is the lock.

We've passed that image
before, just a lock
on a pole, securing
the emptiness.

JOSHUA TREE NATIONAL PARK

The moon lit like any light bulb.
Stars arranged as in a planetarium.
My son says the mountains look
so real they don't look real.
He plays Nintendo in a tent
a quarter mile from the 10
where cars whish by
more naturally
than a flock of birds.

The campgrounds are full
so we're in the outskirts
for those with a lack of foresight,
no 401(k)s or life insurance.
We took wrong turns, wrong jobs
never thinking of tomorrow

and tomorrow is Easter
so the rock climbers
have descended from heaven
with tents and sleeping bags
while I drink Dos Equis
and my wife points out
the dangers of spontaneity.

But I'm convinced I'm outdoors
and the Joshua Tree is my brother.
It endures for half a millennium,
never moves in this breeze, so slight.
No plans, no solutions
for its endangerment, its finish.

Whoever dressed them did it with flair,
with a lyrical stroke, the wish bone trunks
with bushy tips and spiked hair.

The sloth that scattered their seeds
has long since left,
maybe down this road,
looking like any dirt road that recedes
into the imagination,
that promises something is worth seeing

around the bend,
but my legs like frozen trunks
relay messages.
Why go? Who cares?
But I'll care tomorrow

for bosoms and crevices,
elephant-like swells,
bolders tucked into boulders
under the bright sun.
Frowns and mouths sealed in stone.

Our son will yell, *lizard!*
as it scrambles
through granite that will surround us,
waking up the granite within.
I'll mount the highest rock to view
my mimes of indifference,
all named Joshua,
slanting, drooping,
thinking about nothing
in the desert air.

3.

"For sleeplessness, everyone's alone. Every one of us dies young."

— Ralph Angel

SISTER

I'd surrender on the toilet where
the light was strongest. She above me,
searching. She pinched, tweaked.
The blackhead lifted. Precision pressed
on to neck side, ear lobe, a lung or two.
She'd wipe dead cells on my hand.
A cotton ball dipped in alcohol slammed
pores shut.

At night I'd smell the boiling sulfur,
her face covered with steamy towels
by the stove, calming the acne
she measured like tips of enemy heads.
Intimacy vaporized with their departure.
The contours of others emerged
with new tactical demands.

I learned her dread of the pimple and
the comfort of her breathy fingers.
She asked if a girl fucked a guy would
it show on her face? Would others know?
For these questions alone the moon landed.
I'd hear vomiting before each date.
Clusters banded together, pushed
her to the bathroom, retching.

When I drew a ship, she identified the water
then locked herself behind the partition
of our room and studied Latin for days.

BUT DIDN'T ROY ORBISON DIE OF CANCER

Maybe *Pretty Woman*
will shrink a tumor
so I turn up the TV
and she says
with eyes closed,
we could dance to this.

If only.

Look at my tongue,
and she sticks out
an orange pitted coat
nickel thick and I'd lick

those side effects
if she'd ask me,
swallow the crust
while Roy sings

all I can do is dream you.

I pray to the common place
where breath and Roy's voice
begin, beg for the cure
while Roy plans
to squeeze Claudette

to death and my sister
is an hour past
her morphine pill,
but she's out so I lower

*your baby doesn't love
you anymore,*

as Roy's mouth opens
below sunglasses
while the body
hardly budges.

I'M THINKING OF WHAT'S HIS NAME

when he'd crouch
over the pool table
about to take a shot

and nod out

his stick suspended
across the green felt
like a bridge to
something absent

my sister sips tea
head tilts for a nap
cup in the air

jumps slightly
when the phone rings
spills and sobers

in a breeze as
gold leaves lift

I ask if I can zip
her jacket up

remember the bully
who shoved her
and I couldn't budge him
because he was twice
my size and now

with the serenade
of oxycontin
and a tumor
the size of an eight ball

I'm small again

LIKE LOST CHILDREN

Each wants to hold
her but he insists
she sit alone
and the three of us
opposite.
He speaks about what
he knows and doesn't.
Blood fine.
Lungs O.K., but the slow
growing tumor
sprawls on her liver
and prortudes into nerves.
Next was chemo.
No telling if it will work.
My arms tremble slightly
though people
have lived four years
with what she has,
They traveled, biked and
he asks if I have questions.
Did the Celtics make a good trade?
Did the dye in her hair
nose dive to her liver?
Why the liver and not a kidney?
Where do you get a good corn beef sandwich in this town?
Do you have a sister?

WE THINK

this can happen to us
and how will we lie there
when the encroachment
begins? Cysts, tumors
and friends pay their respects,
religiously. Each day
the phone rings with all the love
she couldn't feel.
The eulogy starts before
they lower the body.
Praise heaped
in the hope to keep
her above the boxwoods
in the nurturing cries
as years run into minutes,
as mobility stills.
The catheter attached,
the bed pan in place
and a river of morphine
promises to turn thought
into colorful mush.

A MONTH TO 6 WEEKS
MORE LIKE A MONTH

The nurses model her flowered
Havana, casual dress, the dungaree
jump suit and cut-off

pants. I ask if she's dead and
one says, *she will be.* I quip, *won't you?*
They giggle and explain she's

selling all her clothes for five dollars.
Everything is in boxes and loosely
piled. I enter her room which

is the size of a gymnasium
and she's shorter, suddenly skinny
like Olive Oil in a Popeye cartoon.

She leaps around the bed, all bones
and jumps. I say, *are you ready?*
She remarks, *the nurses are nice*

and I mumble, *not nice. The nurses
aren't so nice.*

FRUGALITY

Vomit the color of green Gatorade
in a thin cream texture, about ten

ounces puddled on a flat pan.
It's as if the cancer asserts, *I'll pick*

the food now. I have no need
for organic yogurt or that lime drink.

She points, *look at the parsley*
from the chicken soup. I pick out

the oxycontin tablet with forty
still inscribed on the upturned

side. She says, *you ran down*
the steps so fast. I don't want you

to hurt yourself. I reply, *it's*
the radiation, the side effects.

A mud slide. A tremor.
I pass her the tab

that goes for a hundred bucks
in Thompkins Square Park and

pour the ginger ale.

I fell asleep and then woke and remembered I have a terminal disease

There's surf in these waters, but the medicine tray
floats. Clear plastic boxes buoy beside

her bed. I worship the little footballs for doing
what I can't. I pass her one, reminisce about

Mrs. Beaver and Zona from the old neighborhood
to distract us from what animals were never

meant to know. When she strokes her liver,
I think of the time we hiked to school and my

younger stomach growled. She advised me
to rub it and I delved below my shirt and that pain

vanished. All the smart decor is baroque compared
to a rented hospital bed, angling in the corner and

the pills need pills. Colors and shapes shift
in my palm. At 8 it's the tan tiny sphere of proterex

and a yellow bit of continex for nausea that
follows. At 9 it's morphine for a constipated

euphoria and 2 orange dots for the sake
of movements. She sips a green concoction,

downs a B and a C with a hesitant gulp.
We laugh when she waves for a taxi

to get out of Cuba, searches the Classified
for her doctor's appointment, but never when

she shivers below a heap of quilts or when
her chin and eyelids droop three stories.

Too much relaxation. A hospice worker
places money on two weeks. Where?

What would we be in two weeks?
Sea weed. Water. And a log afloat.

JET LAG AT THE FUNERAL HOME

The one you only glance at
is groomed and polished.
She didn't signal and you knew this
before you crossed the curtained
area but you're curious and need
to say goodbye to something.
She looks like she looked
and can't object or protect
her body but it's just family anyway,
pacing, circling. Only the pigeon-
toed girl smiles with a goofy smile,
tilts this way and that.
She's the mortician's daughter.
She's seen all the awkwardness
so she daydreams in shifts.
The niece looks and can't,
looks and can't. I inch up
on the face 'til wonder dissolves,
and everything is pasted together,
the cheek, the eyebrow,
greetings and handshakes, all the
wish we could see each other
under different circumstances,
as if there are different circumstances.

BUT IT'S SOLID WOOD

So the Salvation Army and the Jewish Organization
show up simultaneously,

peacefully, and the Jews look like a front
on the prowl for goods to sell privately,

aren't interested in the long dresser.
Neither is the Salvation Army or

"Moving Along," a company on the hunt
for silver platters. No, the dresser stands,

unwanted, stripped of her underwear,
photos, so many patterned scarves,

just a bruise on the left lower drawer,
but still sturdy. The bare reminder

of Max, Morris, Jenny and others
I never knew and when the drawers

are removed it's unrecognizable
like Cliff when a virus took hold of him.

A frame. Bones. And daylight
swinging thru with a disregard for what was.

The superintendent and Juan carry
the lengthy skeleton, that unchanged length,

lift it on a gurney, tilt it in the elevator, down
to the basement, out the side door

and set it on the street
with the trash.

HOW I'D LIKE MY FUNERAL

Clifford Brown improvises from
"Clifford Brown with Strings,"
I'm sealed in a box of four doors,
one splattered blue and beige,
all chipped. It's the door out front
in Venice, CA at right angles
with the glass one from 188 Suffolk Street
on the lower east side in Manhattan
where I celebrated my twenties
and the thin brown one on a single hinge
of Seventeenth Street where my stereo
and toaster were easily stolen.
The thick side entrance
from Montgomery Avenue in the Bronx
completes the box. On second thought,
let's leave one out.
Secure me with an unknown entrance.
I'll wear my lucky-blue underwear,
jeans and a black tee shirt.
A demo reel rolls on a large screen.
First my character from Barney Miller
holds up the police station at gun point
and last, I'll be on the cross as Jesus
in the X-Files. My father cheers
as he never would. His mother
turns sane and conversational.
My mother won't utter a word,
contradicting every impulse
in her suddenly fifteen-year-old body,
straight out of the shapely photo
in front of the fake ocean scrim.
Jimmy Santiago Baca reads my poems,
not reverently, but slowly. Girlfriends

strip and writhe about my coffin.
My wife joins, playing saxophone.
Charlie Parker enters as Sam
scats Happy Birthday.

ACKNOWLEDGMENTS

Special thanks to all those who participated in the Midnight Special Poetry Workshop, the Beyond Baroque Wednesday Night Workshop, and the MFA program at Antioch. Thanks also to Main Street Rag for selecting "Chemical Tendencies" as a finalist for its annual poertry book award.

Some of the poems in this collection were previously published in the following journals and anthologies, occasionally in slightly different form:

Alimentum "B & H Dairy"; *Askew* "Chemical Tendencies"; *Beyond the Valley of Contemporary Poets* "Cravings"; "$2000 for a Ringside Seat", *Mamas and Papas* (City Works Press) "The Unnoticeable Movement of Cloud"; *Echo* "Sister"; *Eclipse* "Going In"; *Foreshock* "Slice of Life"; *New York Quarterly* "But Didn't Roy Orbison Die of Cancer"; *Poemeleon* "Off Broadway"; "Cock"; "Division"; "Sports Bar in Santa Monica"; *Santa Barbara Review* "True"; *Saturday Afternoon Review* "The First Marxist President; *Solo* "Long Beach Aquarium"; *Spot Lit* "Allied Model Train Store"; *Summerset Review* "Phil or Seymour."

ABOUT THE AUTHOR

Paul Lieber's *Chemical Tendencies* was a finalist in the Main Street Rag poetry contest. Paul also won an honorable mention in The Poetry Center's 2010 Allen Ginsberg Poetry Award competition. Paul's poems have appeared in many journals and anthologies. He produces and hosts "Why Poetry" on KPFK radio in L.A. Paul works as an actor and has performed on Broadway, off-Broadway, and in numerous films and TV shows. He holds a B.A. from C.C.N.Y. and an M.F.A. from Antioch University. He lives in Venice, California, with his wife and son.

Visit his website at: **paullieber.com**.

TEBOT BACH
A 501 (c) (3) Literary Arts Education Non Profit

THE TEBOT BACH MISSION: advancing literacy, strengthening community, and transforming life experiences with the power of poetry through readings, workshops, and publications.

THE TEBOT BACH PROGRAMS

1. A poetry reading and writing workshop series for venues such as homeless shelters, battered women's shelters, nursing homes, senior citizen daycare centers, Veterans organizations, hospitals, AIDS hospices, correctional facilities which serve under-represented populations. Participating poets include: John Balaban, Brendan Constantine, Megan Doherty, Richard Jones, Dorianne Laux, M.L. Leibler, Laurence Lieberman, Carol Moldaw, Patricia Smith, Arthur Sze, Carine Topal, Cecilia Woloch.

2. A poetry reading and writing workshop series for the community Southern California at large, and for schools K-University. The workshops feature local, national, and international teaching poets: Wanda Coleman, Amy Gerstler, Patricia Smith, Holly Prado, Dorothy Barresi, W.D. Ehrhart, Tom Lux, Rebecca Seiferle, Suzanne Lummis, Michael Datcher, B.H. Fairchild, Cecilia Woloch, Chris Abani, Laurel Ann Bogen, Sam Hamill, David Lehman, Christopher Buckley, Mark Doty.

3. A publishing component to give local, national, and international poets a venue for publishing and distribution.

Grateful acknowledgement is given to all of our supporters, the Tebot Bach board of directors, Steven R. and Lera B. Smith, and to Golden West College in Huntington Beach, California, all of whom make our programs possible.

Tebot Bach
Box 7887
Huntington Beach, CA 92615-7887
714-968-0905
www.tebotbach.org

This book is set in 10.5 points ITC Giovanni.